# You Matter

## What would living in your purpose everyday look like?

Jamicka Jones

Dr. Sheila Harrison-Williams Thank you very much for your support! I truly appreciate it! You Matter! Blessings, Jamicka Jones

For information:
jamickamotivator@gmail.com
www.jamickajones.com

Copyright © 2014 Jamicka Jones
All rights reserved.
ISBN:1499126417
ISBN-13: 978-1499126419

# DEDICATION

This first book I write and publish; I want to dedicate to my three amazing sons: J'Don, Jamal, and Absalom. You three have given me unconditional love and have not been ashamed to show it to me no matter where we are. You push me, more than you know, to be successful in life so that you will follow the example and always strive for your dreams and learn your purpose early and live in it. You each have been patient with me as I encounter people all over the world and watched me develop a conversation or establish friendships. Many of the stories in the book you lived through and experienced with me. I thank God all the time for blessing & trusting me with three incredibly smart and talented sons to rise as strong men of God. Never give up on your dreams and never stop loving life.

Look at Mommy O,

I'm a living witness of what it looks like!

Love you with all my heart.

## ACKNOWLEDGMENTS

Alma Blount and Anita Willingham, the hours and days you put into reading thoroughly and carefully assisting with the editing process was most important and vital to the accomplishment and success of this book. I could not have taken on this task alone. Your time, patience, friendship, and love mean the world to me. Thank you for your feedback and constructive criticism. You both have shared some major milestone and special memories in my life. Anita, you being at both J'Don and Jamal's birth at Joint Base Lewis Mc Chord and Alma at Absalom birth in Tacoma. It was only fitting that I have two very important women with the name beginning with "A" see me through this project to completion. Jessica Sims, La Trish Thomas, Attallah Cotton, Maria Alexandria, and Megan Lewis; I am so blessed to have served our country alongside you wonderful women in my life. You have encouraged me and supported me while serving in the military, as well as after in civilian life.

Thank you to ALL contributors of the stories in this book! I love you all and so blessed to have had my encounters with you. Summer Sunne'e Carraway Sims, my best friend from childhood and still my best friend today. There's so much I could say about you and our friendship but I'll say this. Since the idea came for me to write a book over 6 years ago, you've said I can do anything and go for it girl! BFF! Adon, Thank you for taking care of our sons while I traveled on speaking engagements, attended many conferences and training to gain more leadership skills, professional, and personal growth. I also appreciate you for allowing me the time I needed to get away from the house to focus on school work and writing this book. allowing me do what is in my heart to do, even though sometimes you may not understand why I'm doing it or when it seemed possible. It truly meant a lot to me.

# CONTENTS

Throughout my travels as a motivational/empowerment speaker, every now and then you come across someone with that certain spark, charm and presence about them. When in their presence it is something you feel that is truly magnetic. You can't quite describe it but you know it when it happens. The year was 1996 and I was the opening keynote speaker for the Illinois FCCLA state conference. FCCLA is an extraordinary student organization preparing young people across America for future success. I was milling around backstage waiting for my sound check and watching the state officers practice their lines for the opening session. Then the organization's student president for that year stepped to the podium and immediately I was struck by her charisma. She had that certain something, a self confidence that comes from knowing who you are and living from that truth. She was bright, vivacious, articulate and self-assured. Needless to say, I was impressed! A few hours later when I finished my opening keynote, that state president came right up to me and in her confident yet genuine way she said, "Hi, my name is Jamicka Edwards and I just loved everything you said and everything you just did and one day I want to do that too!" Well, here I am today, 18 years later and I have the honor and privilege of writing a few words in support of such a remarkable woman who is now out there truly making such a positive impact through her speaking and her book! For those who are lucky enough to hear and experience her words, her passion and her genuine heart, you will be moved by the experience itself. She is the real deal and I am so proud to have her consider me as one of her mentors. One of the qualities I most look for in a speaker or a self help author is someone who "walks the walk & talks the talk" and I know that she certainly does. She is REAL and her compassionate heart is the vehicle of her words. Before I look to follow the advice or strategy of anyone, I first look into who they are by how they live. Well, one needs to look no further with Jamicka because what you see is what you get and what you get is a person with great passion for life, great knowledge for teaching and great experience for leadership! Her life is a beautiful reflection of the woman herself. Once you've had the pleasure of being in her presence either thru her book or a presentation, you will come away feeling inspired to take action in your own life to utilize your personal gifts to affect positive change in this world! Her mission is straight from the heart! I am honored to know her and blessed to call her my friend. I may be one of her mentors, but she is one of my HEROES!

Eddie Slowikowski – Chicago, IL
Empowerment Strategist, Speaker, Author and Consultant

Eddie Slowikowski and me in Springfield, IL at the FCCLA State Conference in 1995 when I first heard him speak.

# PREFACE

Imagine your alarm goes off, you press snooze, and it's still dark outside. Should I sleep a little longer? Yes…. Then you finally get up after the third snooze. You're thankful for waking up another day, yet you want to continue to sleep because you know it's going to be the same normal routine. You think about how the day will go, what you have to get accomplished throughout the day. Your clothes were already prepared the night before. You decided on something a little classy and dressier this day. Today is a new day and you wanted to live in it. You feel like this is going to be different than any other day and you choose to look for how God will present many different opportunities to you and what is in store for you today in your life. Sometimes we live day by day, not knowing our purpose or even caring to know what our purpose in life is or realizing we have a purpose. We go to work to do our job whether it's answering the phone, greeting customers, or answering questions. Perhaps our job has a laid out schedule or routine. We know exactly what it is we will be doing when we arrive at work and the job will be completed in that day. When the clock strikes the time for the end of the day, without any hesitation we are leaving in a hurry to our vehicles to head home. Maybe we have to stop at the gas station and fill up, maybe we have to stop and get fast food, maybe our dinner is waiting for us at the table when we get there but whatever the routine is, that's exactly what it is. … The Normal Routine. We get home, eat, prepare for the next day, sleep, and wake up and start all over again.

I want to share with you some of my personal stories and testimonies from others as an example of what can happen when you wake up believing and knowing you have purpose and recognizing **You Matter**. Even as I type this, the tears of joy are flowing, and I am grateful to God for allowing me to grow into the person He has called me to be. I know that I've been a bucket full of positive encouragement to so many and so many more are in the wings waiting for my smile to brighten their day and my ear to listen to them. I love to be the shoulder to cry on, the person who will hear a cry for help or someone to give that extra boost of motivation that says "You Can Do It!" Some people whom I've gotten to know and live close to will ask, "I need my Jamicka fix, when can we meet up?" I will then look at my calendar and figure out a day and time to meet but what they don't realize is as much as they need a Jamicka fix, I need to be with each and every one of them as well. "Wherever you are it is your friends who make your world"- William James This quote is so perfect for who I am and how I have lived my life. I had no idea the things I did everyday would have such an impact or effect on those I would encounter. How could I know that God was planting seeds all my life to help and guide me and give me such special gifts? I am patient, loving, understanding, energetic, and always eager to meet people from all over the world in many different ways. It is my hope that as I share these mini stories; glimpses into my life and how these moments made a difference in me as well as other's lives that you will be encouraged to know **YOU MATTER**.

Some of the stories will make you laugh, some may bring a tear, and others may have you saying, "Hey, that happened to me too". You may even find yourself thinking how you wish you would have exchanged information with that person you met a few days ago or a few months ago. Don't worry, I promise you, if you allow the door to open, you will be given the chance again when the opportunity presents itself. You will need to keep your eyes and heart open and allow God to send them to you, and this can takes place many times when you least expect it. We are living with a purpose, a dream, a goal, a destiny and once we tap into that purpose there is no telling where our life will take us. To appreciate this journey through testimonies of how one person has lived a life helping to make others know they matter you must understand the background story of my life. It will help you to appreciate even more that anyone, even YOU reading this right now MATTER and you can make a difference in someone's life no matter what your circumstances are, no matter what your background is, or where you came from.

# CHAPTER ONE
# THE UPBRINGING OF JAMICKA JONES

Lucille (Barr) Edwards was born in 1955 and raised in Gary, IN, by her two parents who had a total of twelve children. As a pre-teen, her family packed up and moved to the outskirts of Chicago. Lucille's mother believed in attending church and serving God and He was to be the head of everything. These values were instilled in her family and then later passed on to Lucille's children.

Although Lucille's father smoked cigarettes and drank alcohol on occasion, her mother didn't allow that to stop her from bringing her children to church and training children in the way they should go and not depart from it. *Proverbs 22:6* After graduating from high school, Lucille married and gave birth to her first child, a daughter named Farhonda. Not long after the birth of her daughter, she and Farhonda's father divorced. While living in the suburbs of Chicago, IL, Lucille married James Edwards Jr. in 1977. James came from a much smaller family than Lucille. He was the oldest of four children. He had one brother and two sisters. When James was an adult his father and mother separated and while his mother moved on to another relationship, his father remained without another companion. When Lucille and James married he raised Farhonda, as if she were his own child.

With the union of James and Lucille, she gave birth to her second child, Jamicka, born in 1979 and four years later a third child, a daughter, Anita, born in 1983. The first nine years of Jamicka's life had many sad and troubled moments. The good times, remembered most, were being in church. It was her safe haven to get away from being at home with the yelling, cursing, screaming, and crying. There were times when she wished she was someone else and had a different family because of the lifestyle in her home and the things that happened in her family. As a six year old, she can remember very vividly and clearly some things that took place in her life. She remembers how her mother would try to be a good wife and mother and do things with her girls, while her husband was out in the streets. He worked on cars, got drunk and got high. Most of the time he would do all three only to come home yelling and fighting her mother for no reason at all.

There were many sleepless nights she had to endure and her sisters had to listen to their mother scream and cry in fear of her life (so it sounded to the them). Many times, her father would come and take out his frustration and anger on the girls, and their mother would come in the room and try and protect them, but in trying to stop him, he would beat her even more. Her mother at one time had a black-eye and was bruised. She would have to cover up or tell lies to her mother in order to protect James' character to make him look like he was a different person from what others may have thought. She would say that somehow she inflicted the pain herself because she loved him that much, but yet had a fear of him doing it again. This cycle continued on for as long as Lucille could take it.

In 1989, she finally got enough nerve to leave him and take her girls with her. She escaped to Savanna, IL, one summer never to return to Chicago to live. The move was bittersweet for all, but living in Savanna at the time was Lucille's Aunt also named Lucille. The children were familiar with Aunt Lucille, because from time to time Farhonda and Jamicka would visit in the summer months, over the years, previously. It was definitely a culture shock to move from a predominately black city to a predominately white community and the most affected in the beginning were Farhonda and Jamicka. Farhonda was starting her sophomore year in high school and Jamicka was starting 5th Grade. During that summer, they didn't do too much, but they did attend church services on a regular basis. Jamicka was too young to understand the fact that, everybody at church was not who she would see at school. On her first day of school she was taken aback by the fact that she was the only black student in her class of twenty students. That saddened her greatly and she felt as if she would never make any friends. She went through name calling at times, people making fun of her and on the flip side of that when she would go back to Chicago for visits, she was made fun of. She picked up an accent of sounding proper or some family members would say "white". It used to bother her, but she learned that her more proper sounding voice actually helped her articulate herself more and it was okay to sound different from others.

As time went on throughout Jamicka's childhood from middle school to high school, she was determined not to repeat the life of her mother or her mother's mother, but hoped and prayed to dream for more and to have a better family life of her own someday. Throughout Jamicka's high school life, she chose a different path than that of her other family members. She learned how to set goals and to achieve them with the help of God and having supportive people in her life. She became a member of an organization then called Future Homemakers of America- Home Economics Related Occupations (FHA-HERO), now called Family, Career, and Community Leaders of America (FCCLA). When she started out in the organization she ran for Secretary of her local high school and was voted into that office. The following year she decided to run for a Section Officer as Secretary which was a combination of 7 different high schools. After a speech and good candidacy run, she was voted in. She learned more and more about the organization and was very much involved with it, her community, and the schools in her area. She set a goal to become a State Officer for Illinois State the following year.

Well, in the same year Jamicka was elected as Section Secretary of FCCLA, she was also involved in another high school organization called Business Professionals of America (BPA). Both organizations taught Jamicka how to reach for her goals, how to act in a professional manner at events for school, social events, and evening Galas. She learned how to properly eat with the correct silverware. She learned manners that she had not learned at home, and the proper protocol of how to address business women and men. These organizations and her involvement afforded her the opportunity to meet with Illinois Legislators as well as National Political Leaders in Washington D.C.

In BPA, there were State Officer positions to be filled and Jamicka decided to go for it. Well, she was elected by a combination of 60 different schools in the State of Illinois as the State Vice-President of Special Recognition during her sophomore year going into her Junior Year of High School. In her junior year she did in fact not just run for a State Office for FCCLA, but she ran for the position of State President. She believed that the experience she had gained thus far through FCCLA as well as BPA, she was now ready for the challenge of representing the State of Illinois as President.

After much campaigning over a weekend, a series of questions and answers and a speech in front of over 4000 students, educators, and parents. The votes came in and they elected Jamicka Edwards the State President of the Illinois Association of FCCLA. Not only was this a major accomplishment and achievement for her, but for her to be the first black representation for the State was an even more humbling experience. The invaluable skills she gained while working with these organizations, coupled with having positive role models in her life, have assisted her in blossoming into the business oriented, well spoken woman she is today. In these roles, she was asked to speak at several high schools and judge events for conferences while only being a junior in high school.

Jamicka never felt as though she was very smart academically. In fact her report cards reflected nothing higher than a C the majority of the time. She was an average student and according to the American College Testing Program (ACT) her scores proved that Jamicka would never be accepted into a 4 year University. She did not have family members who completed anything higher than a 2 year degree, so she accepted that she might only be able to go to a Community College or Tech School. This is not the end of the story, but only the beginning of her building confidence, courage, self-esteem, and the ability to set more goals and achieve them while exceeding her own expectations.

Now get ready to see how this has led her to where she is today, not taking no for an answer, not allowing someone to walk away from her without a smile or finding something great out of every day to have purpose and show others purpose and make them believe they matter.

*The following stories are about some of the people who I have met along my journey who have impacted my life, and **Mattered** to me.*

# CHAPTER TWO
# MY BIG SIS

Jamicka "Mickey" Edwards- Jones

What can a sister say? Well, I think I can best describe her as MY baby sister. Although Jamicka and I have not always gotten along (we're a sibling, that's what we do) we've kept a bond that can never be broken.

I remember practicing on my baby dolls hair just so that I could braid Jamicka's hair and put beads on her hair like Serena and Venus Williams, I wanted her to be just as cute as can be. I remember telling Jamicka that I would spank her if she didn't do as I told her (big sister power) but it never happened because she would tell my mom before I could.

When we would have Sunday dinner at Grandma Barr's house and I was "promoted" to the grown up table and Jamicka had to sit at the "children's table", She would always look so pitiful, that I would go ahead and sit with her. I remember the good and the bad, but most of all... I remember the LOVE that was shared in our home.

When I was a freshman in high school, my mom worked two jobs to take care of my sisters and me. We lived one block over from my grandmother in a two bedroom basement apartment and my being the BIG SISTER I had to step up and be an adult when it came to taking care of my sisters at times. If we needed anything beyond my control my grandmother would come over and take care of it. I remember taking a liking to a boy at this age and Jamicka and Anita (our younger sister) told me that they wouldn't tell on me (I had this boy over without permission) if I gave them $5 each. Well, of course I did it and sure enough, they both told my mother. Back then, I didn't know the love that I would have for Jamicka as my younger sister but over the years, I know that a bond like ours could never be broken.

Jamicka has always been motivating and an encouragement to me. When I moved from home and went off to college, the first thing she asked me was "Can I have your room?" I thought it was quite funny because I remember us moving into our three bedroom apartment and I couldn't wait to GET AWAY from her and have my own space. I totally knew that feeling when she asked about having my room I was happy to pass that torch but made sure she knew the "rules". She shook her head in agreement with me of everything I was saying and as soon as I left, she created her own "Big Sister" rules for Anita. She enforced them with signs on her new bedroom door; signs like "JAMICKA'S ROOM or KEEP OUT! ☺

On my visits home from college I saw Jamicka grow into a young lady. She had all the characteristics of being a STRONG and independent young lady. Beautiful, ambitious, eager, aggressive, positive, full of joy, full of life, giving, loving, caring, motivating and so much more. She joined FHA (Future Homemakers of America) in High School and sought to be an officer within the organization. She not only wanted to join, she wanted to be the President of the Savanna High School chapter  Ask me did she accomplish that goal... YES INDEED! She and my mom traveled around to competitions and Jamicka always represented our family well.

When she graduated from high school, Jamicka went to college in Miami, FL and I remember saying "Wow, that's a big city" and I knew if anyone could do it, Jamicka could. She soon afterwards had another goal in mind and that was joining the US Army. Now that one threw me for a loop because she is such a "girly-girl" but wouldn't you know it ... she accomplished that as well. She went through all of the basic training and made it. Jamicka served our country for six years and traveled the world. At such a young age, she didn't know that she was a motivation to me. She gave me something to brag about on a regular basis as well.

Although she didn't complete her degree in Miami, Jamicka didn't let that stop her from all of her dreams. She did graduate from Northwest University in Kirkland, WA with a Degree in Business Management. She did this all while working a full time job and home schooling her children. Okay, talk about getting it DONE. Yep, can you say "YOU GO GIRL?" Oh, and did I mention earlier that she is beautiful? Well, yes she is! She competed a beauty pageant and not only did she motivate others while doing this, she won Mrs. Congeniality. Making friends and building relationships all while just being herself.

To come back full circle, MY SISTER is writing this book and I am so proud of her. Over the last few years she's started this "change of life style journey" and has made such a transformation! She's lost 37 pounds and still counting since having her third son and she's continually encouraging me and others not only to lose weight, but to lose all the heavy weights that have held us back for so many years. No matter what the circumstance, Jamicka has a smile on her face. She lights up a room like no other. She's got the energy and the wherewithal to move mountains and that is called FAITH. I love the faith that my sister has. She took what was a not-so-positive situation and turned her life into one that many will call blessed.

Our grandmother use to say, "You have to play the cards that you're dealt" and I tell you we were not dealt a royal flush but Jamicka has played her cards to the fullest and has won every hand. She does it by continuing to keep God first and knowing that at the end of the day; faith is the substance of things hoped for and the evidence of things not seen. Her faith has taken her so far and God has opened so many doors for her. I'm so proud to say that GOD has shined on Jamicka and her family.

Thank you for your encouragement Jamicka. Thank you for just being YOU! My words of encouragement to you would be my favorite scripture; "For I know the plans I have for you, Plans to prosper and not to harm you, plans to give you hope and a future." – Jer 29:11 your future is looking bright my sister…. REALLY BRIGHT. I love you.

Farhonda Yvette Turner Cullum

My mom and younger sister, Anita at my older sister Farhonda's graduation from American Institute of Business in Des Moines, IA May 1994.

## MY LIL SIS

I don't even know where to begin about my sister Jamicka. She's wild and crazy and loves to have fun. She has the biggest heart and is always looking for a way to help others. She's always been there for me and even when we were younger and would fight, we still loved each other and stuck up for the other. The older we got the closer we became and she was always there for me to tell me the truth even if it did hurt for a little bit.

Once she graduated from high school she would come back and surprise me at school. I felt so special and so loved because my sister was the coolest graduate I knew. She reminds me all the time how beautiful I am and how much I mean to her and that really means a lot to me. She would write me the best letters when I went to basic training and if no one else would write me, I knew she would. After she had her first, son J'don, I got a message saying she had him and I cried so hard because he was my first nephew and I couldn't be there to hold him, but soon after, the letter came with pictures of my beautiful nephew.

After graduating from Army Basic Training, I immediately flew out to Washington to be there with them. Sometimes she's more of a mother figure to me because through all the things I've been through, she's the one that seemed to care the most and was there to comfort me.

I have to thank her for convincing me to take my assignment to Germany It was one of the best times of my life and taught me so much. God works in the most awesome ways because out of all the duty stations in Germany, we ended up only an hour away from each other. She didn't hesitate to come see me as soon as that plane landed. She helped me clean my barracks room, got me a blanket, and even toilet tissue. If I hadn't gone to Germany I wouldn't have met my husband and have my two beautiful kids.

My sister deserves all the greater things in life and when things aren't right in her life I feel it too. I want to make it right and do everything I can to change her situations. Once I realize that I can't I just pray that God will see her through it. When she's sad I'm sad, when she cries I cry, and when she is rejoicing so am I! I'm so proud of her for never giving up on her dreams, for always letting me come along to all the fun things she did when I was younger, and for always being there for me. I love you so much Mickey!

Your Sister Nita Bugg

07/16/2005

My younger sister and me at one of our most memorable times, having the opportunity to live in Europe at the same time and experience Germany together.

# CHAPTER FOUR
## TWINS

*You're never too young to make long lasting true friendships. This next story is about a lady who came into my life and has stayed in my life for more than 25 years.*

Come with me to a time when as a 10 year old you attend church with your mom and siblings. You attended every church service from Sunday School, Sunday Service, Tuesday night Prayer, Wednesday night Bible Study, Thursday night Choir Rehearsal, and all night Shut-In's. The only time you didn't attend church was when you were extremely sick because being only a little bit sick meant you still attended church and you went to the alter for special prayer. Sometimes you'd feel better and sometimes it seemed the prayers didn't work but you still went to church. You often fellowship with many other churches and support their programs such as Pastor Anniversary, Choir Anniversary, Youth Revivals and so much more.

On one particular Saturday service, my church home, which was located in Savanna, IL went to support a church service in Milwaukee, WI. It was a cold winter evening as we traveled the 300 miles to Milwaukee. After the long bus ride the young ladies were anxious to get to the bathroom quickly because our moms had rollers in our hair and we needed to get ourselves fixed up.

We'd have socks on our feet over our stockings and have our tennis shoes or house shoes on. We couldn't wait to touch up the lip gloss on our lips so we could look our best. We primped and primed in the mirror until our mothers pulled us out of the bathroom.

For me a very special meeting occurred in the bathroom. As I did my last look over in the full length body mirror I immediately looked to my right to see a beautiful woman standing next to me wearing the exact same outfit. I smiled so big and if it was silent you could hear the saliva sound swish. We both had on a beautiful white button down blouse, navy blue skirts, navy blue belt with gold around the buckle. I just couldn't stop smiling and thinking to myself who is she? Where did she come from? Wow, we're dressed alike and we don't even know each other. We exchanged eye contact, she looked me up and down and with a smile on her face said "Nice outfit twin".

She had the most gorgeous smile and beautiful white teeth and her accent had a little country twang to it. I felt so good in that moment and I knew right then I liked her and I wanted to be her friend. It didn't matter that she was much older than me. I just felt an instant connection with her. We sat by each other during the church service and exchanged phone numbers and mailing addresses. During our conversation, I discovered her country accent came from her residing in Hartshorne, Oklahoma. At that time the only way to communicate long distance was by landline.

Sometimes talking on the phone could be very expensive depending on the location and the length of time you talked. Because of this we mostly communicated via snail mail. We wrote each other letters and sent each other cards all the time. We promised we would see each other again. She traveled from Oklahoma to Wisconsin for that church service, but I felt like God brought her all that way for me. Although 12 years separated us in age, we didn't allow that to have an effect on our friendship. She was there for me in many ways and throughout my life she never forgot about major milestones in my life. She even traveled to Illinois for my eight grade graduation ceremony. 25 years later, we still write letters- she has the most beautiful handwriting ever. We mostly email now and hardly ever get to speak on the phone but we are always in each other's hearts and we know that no matter what we will never forget how we met and our dressing alike. The exchange of many letters and phone calls over the years got us both through a lot in our lives and I will forever be thankful for my friendship with Cherie' Battle.

# CHAPTER FIVE
# AN ADOPTED FATHER FIGURE

*Catfish was a favorite of mine to have after a great friend returned from a fishing trip. Please enjoy the story from a man who means a lot to me. – Catfish George*

First off I want to thank God for placing such a wonderful little girl into my life some 30 or more years ago who has become a deep, deep part of my life and family. I was stationed in Savanna IL, back in the late 1990's at the Savanna Army Depot. When my children moved to join me there from North Carolina and were enrolled in school they met Jamicka and her sisters. My oldest daughter, Shaneice, was around the same age as Jamicka so they visited on base and they became friends. For some special reason, only thru God, Jamicka was drawn to me, I believe, due to the way I loved my children, gave them my attention, and played with them and most of all my catfish. Cooking was my pastime and Jamicka loved to eat. As time went on and we got to know each other better, we became as close as family can get.

Jamicka was a little girl with the absence of knowing a real Dad's love and attention. It was just she and her mom and sisters. As the years passed she always wanted to be around my girls and me because we always had fun over at my place. I loved cooking for them. Most of all I let children be children. My time was up at the Army Depot and I was retiring from the military. My family and I moved back to North Carolina.

Some years passed and I was adjusting to civilian life. I did not know the impact I really had on this special little lady but she never forgot me or my children. As she was coming into young adulthood, college,and military life. Jamicka found my daughters and kept in contact with them. One day I got a call from her while she was working in a hotel and I was so happy to hear from her. The imprint left on my heart of this sweet little girl, now young lady, sounding so happy as if she had found her long lost father. I still get happy knowing that I was thought of by this young lady and she seems to have a love for me.

Jamicka has remained in contact over the years and updated me on what happens in her life. As an adult she never failed to call me when she needed to talk through life's challenges. Jamicka later got married and has three wonderful children. The most amazing thing is I am the grandfather to her children. She let me know each time she was going to bring a bundle of joy into the world. I thank God for allowing me to share those moments in her life. My job as her stand in father was to encourage, praise, strengthen, and support my daughter the best way I could, LISTEN to her and give the best advice I could. She has grown into such a wonderful woman, mother, believer in Jesus Christ, and loving wife to whom I am so proud to be a Dad to. I love her for all her accomplishment and even more for all her failures (few). One of the most beautiful gifts God has given me is that I can I call her DAUGHTER.

George Miller- Phoenix, AZ

# CHAPTER SIX
# SHOE CARNIVAL

*You'd never think that a shoe salesman could become a best friend. Well this next story is exactly what takes place.*

My mother has loved to shop and dress-up perfectly matching her clothing with shoes. Her closets have always been filled with all types of shoes. A few times a year my mom would take me and my two sisters shoe shopping usually before school started and after income tax time if there was extra money. Due to her being in the area so often attending college she discovered one of the best places to shop for shoes in the Quad Cities called Shoe Carnival. It was time for back to school shopping and we made a stop at Shoe Carnival. When you typically walk into Shoe Carnival you first hear fun music being played, bringing you to the mindset of being at an actual carnival. There are jams you know and recognize, and you want to dance and party as soon as you hear the music. You then see a big wheel that can spin with different discounts on it $5 off, $10 off, buy 2 get 1 pair free, deals like that. This is the tactic often used to get customers to buy multiple pairs of shoes. When you go into Shoe Carnival you are leaving with at least three or four pairs of shoes even if you came in, initially, for one specific pair of shoes.

My mom introduced us to this young handsome white guy with pretty brown eyes. If you know anything about Lucille Barr-Edwards, it's that she's super friendly and some might even call it very flirtatious. This sparkling young man was very eager to meet us and as my mom said "Hi Duwayne, these are my girls", we all just smiled and got caught up in his smile back at us. He was a very attractive young man. I think my mom was impressed that he could remember our shoe size. He even got to know some of the shoe styles we were drawn to and selected similar styles and colors to see if we would like those as well, marking shoe prices down to help encourage an even bigger sale.

Then all of a sudden, the volume of the music will mute and you'd hear over the loud speaker – "$20 off when you purchase $100 or more in shoes. Come find an associate right now to get this special offer for you". Of course, you can imagine the voice was very pleasing, fun, and exciting and made you want to find the associate not only for the discount but to see who was talking. That voice was the young brown eyed salesman who became another great friend of mine and the big brother I never had. He has remained in my life for over 25 years, Vern Duwayne Owens Jr.

Since first meeting Duwayne he has become more than the salesman who hooked my family up with great deals on shoes. He's had an active role in my life supporting things I did throughout high school, college, and into adulthood. I could call on him for advice. As a teenager starting to date young guys, he was sure to follow up to see how it was going. When a break up occurred and I was hurting, he also felt my pain but would reassure me, that Meka would be fine and there was a good guy out there for me.

While in high school, I was very active and involved in the organization previously called Future Homemakers of America/ Home Economics Related Occupations (FHA-HERO), now called Family, Career, and Community Leaders of America (FCCLA). In the State of Illinois our big annual State Conference is always held in Springfield, IL. This is not too far from where Duwayne resides so sometimes he'd come and visit me while I was there attending a conference.

We often times say it's a small world and you never know just how small it is until you run into someone you know that knows someone you know through another source. While attending a state conference for FCCLA one year, there was a group of students who stopped by my hotel room and one of them happened to be Duwayne's younger brother. Duwayne didn't realize his brother was involved in the organization and Adam, his brother would have not expected to see his brother there. Adam resided in Chenoa, IL and he and I became friends. Adam asked me to be his date for prom that year and it was a lot of fun having the experience of attending prom at a different high school. Although Adam and I lost contact after we graduating from high school, my friendship with Duwayne has only grown stronger over the years.

There was a time in Duwayne's life that he went through some experiences and situations that were not so good, but I'd like to believe our conversations over the phone and a few visits helped him to remain strong for his two children at the time. As an adult I lived in different states for college and the military. No matter the miles or distance that separated us he has remained a great friend to me.

Jamicka & Duwayne in 1995

# CHAPTER SEVEN
# THE BEAUTICIAN

*When I'm home visiting in Chicago my hair is styled by two women. One of whom was able to see me grow from a pre-teen to adulthood and still does my hair when I visit home.*

I've known Jamicka most of her life. She was still in high school when I first met her and her mother Lucille who, by the way, is one of my best friends today. Even in high school she was a shining star that was so bright. Her friends looked like the colors of a rainbow...they were black, white, and all shades, with smiles and hopes for bright futures.

Back in the mid 80's & 90's, I owned a salon called Crystal Images. It was located in Rock Island, Illinois which is about 40 miles from their home in Savanna IL. I was attending Way of Life Ministries and ministering on the Praise Team at that time. My pastor was going there to speak and he asked the Praise Team to go with him to do praise and worship. That was when I met Jamicka. She was there with her mother and they were on fire for the Lord, working faithfully with their church and pastor. After church we spoke, I encouraged her and at the same time was encouraged by her. Even then I knew that she was someone special. God had a plan for her life. I gave them my business card and invited them to come to my salon in Rock Island.

I was delighted when Jamicka called me for an appointment to come to the salon. They became regular clients and we became so close that I was included in many of their family events. I was there for graduations, church programs, and birthdays. I've stayed overnight at their home and even helped coordinate Jamicka's wedding rehearsal along with doing hair for everybody.

When I got married and moved to Chicago with my husband Keith, I kept begging her mother Lucille to move to Chicago too. The girls had all grown up, gone to the military, gotten married and moved out of Savanna. I knew they had family in the Chicago area, and even though I'd closed my salon in Rock Island and moved back to Chicago, Jamicka would still search me out to take care of her hair. We would manage to keep in touch, praying and encouraging each other along the way. Whether it was in my kitchen or at any salon where I've worked at in Chicago, this girl would find me. It was funny; because she could find me anywhere I was located. I believe she had radar on me, whether she found me for hair or for prayer, the bond we shared was not going to be broken.....it was sealed by God.

These days I'm teaching Cosmetology and Aesthetics so I only have a few choice clients that I personally service. It goes without saying that Jamicka will always be one of them-no matter the miles or the years that separate us.

God has called both of us into ministry, and His plan for Jamicka has allowed her to serve her country in the military, to travel the world, to marry a wonderful man (even if it wasn't my son), to be a wonderful mother to three amazing boys, to be a pageant queen, to teach, and now to write a book. She leaves her mark everywhere she goes, and the light of Christ shines bright in her life. When you see her, you see the love of God in her and she freely gives it to all she meets.

That's why I will always love Jamicka and her family...they have become MY FAMILY. Love you Mickey!

Grace and Peace be Multiplied unto You, Love Always

Evangelist Crystal Hudson-Jones Chicago, IL

# CHAPTER EIGHT
# LASTING IMPRESSIONS

*Who could have imagined two girls who started out in 5$^{th}$ grade as classmates, but would become great friends and remain in each other lives no matter the distance?*

I first met Jamicka while attending primary school in a very small town in Northwest Illinois. We did not have an instant friendship and our friendship was not always as strong as other friendships I had during the years. As we got older though, our friendship continued to grow. When we reached high school, Jamicka was very active in many clubs and organizations. She was in the Drama Club, Band (I pushed my own daughter towards the bass clarinet in band because I remember how well Jamicka played and how much she enjoyed it), Yearbook Staff, and she was even the FHA State President. Oh, and we can't forget being voted Best Dressed her Senior Year.

I always admired Jamicka's determination. Being from such a small town, we did not have a lot of diversity in our schools growing up. She never let that keep her from achieving her goals. After high school, my family moved out of state and I soon began to lose touch with many of my old friends. Jamicka was one friend, that no matter how long we went without talking, we could pick up a conversation as if we still saw each other every day.

Throughout the years we have been able to keep in contact through phone calls, email and social media. One thing I have learned is that family is incredibly important to Jamicka. She supported her husband as they traveled for his career. She also wanted her boys to have the best opportunity at succeeding. She took on the task of homeschooling them when she felt the public education system was failing her children.

When she decided to put them back into a public school, I know how difficult a decision that was for her. She met with teachers, administrators and other parents to ensure that the school was right for her boys. Jamicka has always been career driven. She doesn't take a job for a paycheck. She finds a job that is the perfect fit for her and one that she knows will allow her to thrive.

Whether she was working with a direct sales company or in the schools, she made sure that her professionalism came through at all times. Personally, Jamicka makes sure that she has time to care for herself. By working out and eating right, she has been a real inspiration to me while reaching her weight loss goals. Jamicka is someone that I looked up to in high school and still look up to, today. She is a wonderful wife and mother and I am especially blessed to be able to call her a friend.

Brienne Matthews- High School Classmate- Georgia

## CHAPTER NINE
## MY ROAD DAWG

*Not everyone can handle a silly, wild, outgoing girl. This friend did and she still loves me the same today.......*

I have a friend named Jamie Lynn Bailey Schroder. We attended Savanna High School together and this friendship has blossomed over time but I will start at the point of my sophomore year and her freshman year in high school. We didn't start out as close friends, but we got to know each other through seeing each other in the halls and at school sporting events. She was usually smiling and laughing with another girl named Angie. Over time I learned she liked to go dancing just as much as I did and we would go out to places where we could dance together.

When the store named Pamida reopened in our town, I worked there along with Jamie and two other friends named Angie and Stefanie. The four of us hung out after work hours but it was Jamie and I who really did a lot of the road trips together. I can remember a time we took a road trip to Peoria, IL for Boys State Basketball. Our mothers trusted us enough to go there for two days and even stay in a hotel alone. Our road trip was going great but on the way to the tournament I was speeding just a bit. Okay, a lot. I believe I was going about 85 in a 60 mph zone. I spotted a police car on the opposite side of the highway so Jamie began to panic. I said to her, "Girl I got this." I knew the policeman was going to take the next ramp to come around to get me, so I drove faster to get off the ramp and pulled off to the side of the road. I turned off my headlights and we sat for a while cracking up laughing because that's what we did together. I knew that if I had been ticketed that I deserved it because I was speeding.

So on our way back home, I was doing it again. "Lead Foot" had become my nickname. I was speeding again and this time I was caught. Luckily, I was only going 15mph over the speed limit so I had two choices: 1) pay the ticket or 2) show up for driving school and the ticket would be erased from my record. I took the second choice and guess who went back to Central Illinois with me? My road dawg Jamie.

We loved to listen to the music and just talk. I was so thankful she was willing to come to that long boring six hour driving school class. I can remember her doodling on paper while we were there in a class full of young teenagers who were caught disobeying the law but given a second chance to get it right. Jamie ended up truly being the friend for me I needed especially while in high school during an important time for every senior - Prom. I didn't really have a boyfriend in high school, nor did I date anyone. It seemed I always had long distance friendships that never lasted and locally the guys just weren't into a relationship with me. At first I wasn't going to attend my senior prom, but Jamie said she'd go with me and be my date. What a great friend! So I was able to pick out a cute purple dress and Jamie got hers. We rode together to Buck's Barn, where Prom was held for many years for our school. My mom showed up and took a few pictures. It was a fun time, but the best was "After Prom." This was held back at the high school and the Junior Class parents had the school set up Casino Style for us. Most people changed into comfortable clothes and Pajamas. Jamie and I changed into our Pajamas. We gambled with fake money, sumo wrestled, watched movies, and played other games. There were many prize drawings at the end of the night. I won a TV/VHS combo and a cordless phone both of which I took to college with me.

After graduation, it was the traditional for seniors to have a graduation party/reception and it was usually hard to juggle to be at other senior class members' so they were held throughout the weekend. Mine was immediately after the graduation ceremony and it was held at my church in the dining hall. Although there were other senior parties going on, Jamie chose to be there at mine with me and sat at the head table right next to me. This was so important to me and meant the world to me that I was at the top of her list. All of my family knew how important she was to me.

Over the summer Jamie and I still remained pretty close and got to know each other even more. We made our final road trip together as teens to Six Flags Great America in Gurnee, IL. It was myself, Jamie, our friend Angie, and my best friend Summer. Summer lives in Chicago so we went to pick her up on the way to Six Flags. Jamie and I even had matching outfits and swimsuits we purchased from our job, Pamida, that we wore at the park on the first day. We talked about our future plans and remaining in touch in the future.

The first college I attended was Johnson & Wales University, Miami, Florida in August 1997 after graduation. Jamie had always said she wanted to live somewhere sunny and possibly Florida, so she went with my mom, my younger sister and myself to Miami to see me off to begin college. It was the sweetest graduation gift ever and our lives would begin to be separated by distance but never from the heart.

Four years later my younger sister graduated from high schools, which lead to my visit back to Illinois so we would be reunited back in our hometown. We were both pregnant at the same time with our first child. Shortly after my visit home to Illinois, I received a phone call from my friend Jamie that she lost her baby. I was so devastated for her and really saddened in my heart because although I was still going through my pregnancy it made me sad that she was no longer pregnant and the child she was carrying didn't make it.

God has a way of letting us know what he is doing and even when we can't fully see the picture. When he reveals it later, there is no denying anything was a mistake or wasn't supposed to happen. A few years later, Jamie met her true love and is married to an awesome man of God who loves Jamie more than himself. They have been blessed with an amazing son who has looks like both Jamie and her husband with gorgeous dimples to add to that.

We have to always trust in God and know that his timing is always perfect and although something may not fully develop or come to pass when we think, we can't stop believing in what he has for our future. As time has gone on, Jamie and I remain in touch, 17 years later, through text messages, phone calls, and yearly family letters and pictures. Even though we don't get to speak often, I believe as we get older our love for each other is strengthened more by our commonality in God, family, and people. She made her home in the sunny state of Florida and now I'll always have a friend to visit.

I am forever Thankful for her not only being my date to Senior Prom, going on many road trips with me, and being that lifetime friend that is so hard to find and that you never want to lose. When you have that don't take it for granted and don't lose it.

Me and Jamie in Miami, FL just before I started my first college

## CHAPTER TEN
## FINDING THE GOOD IN EVERY SITUATION

*Not every friendship will last. You have to remember, people come into your life for a reason, a season, or a lifetime. Enjoy whichever one it is and learn to let go when it's time.*

Sometimes in life we will make friends with someone and just know instantly you have clicked. You believe in your heart that no matter what your relationship will withstand the test of time. I want to tell you about someone that came into my life while attending junior college in Iowa.

I studied business at a small two year college called American Institute of Business (AIB). While living in the dorm, I became friends with a girl in one of my business classes. We got to know each other through the class and she shared with me that her current roommate was moving out and she was looking to get an apartment off campus. I was ready to get out of the dorm myself and thought it would be a great idea to live together. Once the semester was over, we moved in with each other and we found we had even more in common than we thought.

We loved our apartment to be spotless. We kept our space clean. When we decided to go shopping for our bathroom, we instantly fell in love with the same color scheme   purple and gray. We both were working while attending college so some evenings we spent time together and others we did our own thing. We were the same size in clothing so we were able to borrow each other's clothes often.

Sometimes we didn't know one had borrowed the other's clothes until both of us came home from work and saw each other. We weren't bothered by it because we both kept everything together. Occasionally, we went out together for dinner or dancing. I felt we got to know each other very well and understood boundaries set forth in our living arrangements and in our personal lives. Suddenly things begin to change and because I don't have her permission to go into detail, I won't. I will say this, although I felt like some things that happened crossed the line in our friendship, after I moved out I forgave her.

We met up in person just before I left for Army Basic Training. She came to my hotel to see me off and what do you know, we would have on the same pair of white and navy blue ADIDAS tennis shoes. I had just purchased them as my running shoes for Basic Training at one store and she purchased hers because she liked them and planned to run in them. We hugged each other and promised to stay in touch. I wrote to her a couple times while at Basic Training and Advanced Individual Training and she wrote to me a few times. We went a year without talking and the last time I remember talking to her was just after I got married in 2000. Although we said we would stay in touch, I believe that our friendship changed. I oftentimes look back to the fun times we had together as college roommates and can see the good in those times and will not regret that and appreciate her being in my life for that season.

# CHAPTER ELEVEN
# THE UNITED STATES MARINES CORPS

*Sometimes the goals and plans we lay out don't end up the way we think but if we keep living with a purpose, it may come back around to us in a different way.*

When I was a senior in high school I thought I had all my plans together. Recruiters for all of the military branches usually will come to the high schools at certain times of the month during our lunch period to talk to students. Their hope was to spark interest in students who didn't know anything about the military or to re-connect and follow up with those who may have shown some interest previously. They brought in T-shirts, ink pens, bumper stickers, and key chains. After two trips to our nation's capital in Washington, D.C, I fell in love with the President's Marine Corps Band. I saw myself in the perfectly cut beautiful green grass they marched on playing in the hot sun for people all over the nation. If you've never experienced watching and listening to the Marine Corps Band, I highly recommend it at least one time in your life. After watching them I knew I was going to join the United States Marine Corps.

When the recruiter came to me and asked "Have you thought about joining?" I quickly said with a big smile on my face "YES! I will. What do I need to do?" A few weeks later I went to the processing center in Chicago. It was an overnight stay and I even made some new friends while I was there. I completed a physical exam and I also took an ability test called the ASVAB (Armed

Services Vocational Aptitude Battery) which was conducted to determine my qualification and job classification.

I passed the ASVAB and had a set date to leave for Basic Training at Camp LeJune, NC, shortly after high school graduation. That winter I had a conversation with a friend who was serving in the Marines and she shared her Basic Training experience with me. One thing I wasn't expecting her to tell me was that you had to jump in a 10 feet deep pool with your rifle. 10 feet deep?! Really?? I was then and still now to this day terrified of swimming due to a traumatic experience as a child.

> *My father had me and my older sister out in a pool. We were on an inflatable raft and he was playing around with us. He kept tipping it back and forth and he kept laughing. I wasn't laughing and I didn't find anything about it funny at all. I think my older sister was laughing. Well tip, tip, topple. We flipped over into the water and I went down. I thought I was going to die. I couldn't breathe, I couldn't see, I didn't know what to do. I was so mad at my father in that moment and for the rest of the day. He didn't know that this experience, at the age of 8, would affect me for the rest of my life.*

That day flashed back in my mind as I attempted to listen to my friend's adventures of her experience. There wasn't any way I was going into the Marines now! I can't swim! So I did what any person would do that has a fear of something, I said forget that and I quit. I

made other plans for after high school. I applied for a college in Miami, FL – Johnson & Wales University. I was accepted and planned to begin in the fall of 1997.

On the day my recruiter came to pick me up for Basic I didn't open the door. I pretended to not be home and since I was home alone it was pretty easy to avoid going to the door. I could see his tall stature through the white see through curtains at the back door. I peeked over the couch that allowed you to see from the living room through the kitchen to the backdoor. He stood there for a minute and I thought to myself, 'Is this man ever going to leave?' He rang the doorbell again. I waited patiently. He still stood there. He then began to knock. I wanted there to be a voice to him from the outside to say, "She's not home, and she's not going to Basic Training so leave now." Finally after three minutes but what felt like an hour, he left. I thought, 'Yes, I'm in the clear. No drowning in the water with a weapon for me!' I went on with my life thinking the recruiter didn't care either way so I blocked it out of my mind. Now I know that if you have ever served any military service time or if you were or are a recruiter you may be calling me some names right now.

Let me finish before you think of me so negatively. As life would have it, I still would have an opportunity to proudly serve my country in the United States Army. After attending college for a year and a half I decided to do something different so I signed up and quickly left for Basic Training at Fort Jackson, SC. It was extremely hot, tons of bugs, and lots of PT- Physical Training. Because I had life experience outside of high school and some college credits I was able to come into the Army with the rank of PFC- Private First Class. I came into the Army with a different mindset and a higher level of maturity than that of many of my Battle Buddies. Many of the soldiers looked up to me for comfort and guidance as this was for some their first time away from home and family. The Army taught me values such as Loyalty, Duty, Respect, Selfless Service, Honor, Integrity, and Personal Courage. There were so many life lessons I learned while serving my obligation. I met some amazing people, some who I still keep very near and dear in my heart and have great personal relationships. The military has a way of bringing people together from all different backgrounds, nationalities, and cultures. Even through our differences, we all become a family. You learn to lean on each other through, the worse times in your life, but you also share some of your proudest and greatest moments in life.

Once you're trained working fully in your MOS- Military Occupational Skill, and begin to go through the ranks of certifications, passing inspections, going to the field, deployments, and PCSing – Permanent Change of Station there are so many opportunities you can experience and have the chance to go through. I built strong and lifelong friendships while serving on Active Duty and as a military spouse that have been truly valuable in my life and without those relationships and experiences I wouldn't be who I am

today. Without my journey leading me to the US Army, I would not have met the father of our three amazing sons.

Anita Willingham and myself in our Supply Room. She was not only my Army Supervisor but she would encourage me to finish college through the Army taking advantage of many opportunities as a Soldier. Later she would help me with my Resume as I transitioned into the Civilian world after leaving the Army. Lastly, Anita was one of the Editors for this book and spent many hours with me on the phone, on the computer, and guiding me through this project and in life. Thank you Anita, My Mentor for life!

# CHAPTER TWELVE
# FUEL THE FORCE

*We are always able to learn from each other through our life experiences.*

I met Jamicka during the fall of 2000. We were initially connected through mutual military friends and associates at Fort Lewis, WA at a time when we were young enlisted soldiers. Regardless of the physical distance from each other and where life has taken us, we've grown closer. Jamicka is one of those friends that you might go days, months or even years without seeing her, but once you do catch up it's like you never missed a single moment.

I cherish our friendship because as we've grown in life, we've shared ideas, experiences, and encouraged each other through good and uncertain times. I feel so blessed to have a friend who is not judgmental, but rather honest, thoughtful and extremely kind. She understands how life can get so busy because we're desperately trying to take care of others and ourselves. She never ceases to amaze me with her own flexibility as a mother, wife and a professional.

I admire how she is able to balance her obligations and find the time to enjoy the pleasures of life such as a day at the park with the kids or a simple bike ride on a sunny day! Jamicka is truly an inspiration to me and someone to emulate. She reminds me of how normal it is to be so busy, yet at the same time she demonstrates the importance of taking the time, even if only a moment, to enjoy the simple pleasures of life.

CW3 Veronica Spell- Fort Eustis, VA

Meeting the whole Spell Family for the first time in Arlington, VA July 2013. Veronica and I kept in touch so much that it felt like I already had known her husband and daughter.

# CHAPTER THIRTEEN
# SISTER 2 SISTER INTERNATIONAL

*When you are a blessing to others, God will bless you! Don't do it to expect a blessing, just do it because you are already blessed.*

The year escapes me, but the event was Living His Word's annual Christmas around the World, a women's ministry event hosted at my home. She was invited and introduced to me by a mutual friend. I do not recall how much we interacted that evening, just that it was a great time with lots of laughter from everybody. Though we did not establish a BFF relationship that night, she contacted me some time later (cannot remember if it was weeks or months later) and asked if her family could stay with me for a spell, which was made up of her sister-in-law, her 2 baby boys and Jamicka. She was in the process of transitioning from Washington to Germany with her husband. Though I did not really know Jamicka well, I felt like I did, and was quite comfortable with the request. She had a lot going on to prepare to leave, as I did with work and school.

So I only remember brief encounters when she was here. However, it was clear that a life-long friendship was formed. Our friendship evolved over time as Jamicka periodically contacted me from abroad. I know that much of our conversations were spent catching up on how each other's family was doing. But I vividly remember her expressions of gratitude for me allowing her family to stay in my home.

Eventually, their family returned to WA. Jamicka started to attend functions for LHW Women's Ministry again. Our friendship evolved into a sisterhood. In 2007, I wrote a book and launched an independent women's ministry. I only have memories of her commitment to both. I remember Jamicka pushing and promoting both causes as though they were her very own. The dedication she displayed was priceless. The following year I hit some hard times, my mother passing and new challenges in my marriage. While I retreated, I can still remember her reaching out. For a period of time, we had little communication, but mutually maintained an inner commitment to our sisterhood. It has just been in the past year that God has brought it all full circle. And here we are...on the heels of your first book being written!

In His Service,

Yolanda Perry- Spanaway, WA

# CHAPTER FOURTEEN
# BAMBERG, GERMANY

*Some church sisters will teach you and encourage you and then there will come a time when you will have to encourage them. This friend is a friend for life and we have encouraged each other along our journey together.*

On the day I met Jamicka Jones, I was going into the Chapel on Bamberg Army Post. I can't remember the exact date. Jamicka was walking up to the chapel with a double stroller and the two oldest boys were strapped inside. Jamicka was coming to the chapel to gain information about the chapel hours for church services.

I noticed that she was walking towards me and I spoke to her, and Jamal, her middle son, was the cutest little man. He had two fingers in his month and he looked like the squishiest little baby ever. He loved his mama; he did not want to be out of her sight. I asked her if I could help her, and she replied, "I just wanted to see what services were here."

We began to talk about the church service and the hours and times that we held the services for the Church of God In Christ Services. We also began to just talk, and she was there because her husband was in the Army, as was mine. Both our husbands were active duty. As time went on, I discovered that my new best friend Jamicka is the most talented, well rounded person. She is the most down to earth magnificent friend/family that anyone could ever hope to have.

Antoinette Turman- Fort Lee, VA

## CHAPTER FIFTEEN
## MP, PLEASE DON'T GIVE ME A TICKET

*Making new friends at the most awkward times and moments is my life story. This one you will find very interesting and it is all true! That's me Jamicka Jones. Don't try this at home.......*

It was May 2004 in Bamberg Germany when I met Mrs. Jamicka Jones. At the time I was a Military Police officer in the Army. While working the road one evening doing patrol work, I noticed a red Jeep Cherokee rolling in the parking lot of the movie theater with a person standing on the back bumper. I turned on my flashers and proceeded to initiate a traffic stop. When I turned on my lights, the vehicle stopped immediately. I exit my vehicle and proceed to make contact with Ms. Tamara Jones (Jamicka's Sister-In-Law). Tamara was the person on the back of the SUV, riding there because apparently Jamicka was playfully threatening to leave her at the gas station. This was a funny situation and an even funnier story. I proceed to the car and start to talk to Jamicka to let her know that this was a post safety violation, and a very unsafe act. After warning the two of them, I noticed that there were two small children in the back seat of the car; boys. Jamicka, being the person that she is, engaged me by asking me where I was from. I told her that I was from Chicago, IL. She took a huge gasp of air, and said "I AM TOO!!!" I said, "Really, what part?" she told me of the area that she was from and I spoke more of the area that I was from.

About a week or so after this, I had run into Jamicka again in the PX along with Tamara and the boys. Come to find out these were some lively little guys that loved being outside in the mix of things and having fun. At this time Jamicka and I shared a conversation more about Chicago, and how much we miss the food, and overall Chicago culture. We exchanged numbers and kept in contact from that day forward. Jamicka turned out to be an awesome person, and we are still in contact to this day. Jamicka is literally like an angel here on earth amongst humans, a woman of God and an outstanding motivator. Jamicka has always been someone that I could speak to about anything good or bad. It seems as if she has a result or solution to any problem. Jamicka is also an amazing homemaker. Her husband and boys have always been first in her life. On top of all these things; she has managed to secure so much formal education and continues to make things happen.

Changing lives one by one, Jamicka is a pure icon in her community and is capable of changing the view of anyone seeing anything in a negative light. Furthermore, Jamicka plays a pivotal part in the life of anyone that she encounters. I love Jamicka a ton, and would never take back a moment lived in her presence.

God Bless

Ron Carter- San Antonio, TX

# CHAPTER SIXTEEN
# FROM ABORTION TO NEW BEGINNING

*Sometimes you never know how you were a blessing to someone and may not find out until 10 years later like I did. This young lady has a testimony to share. Learn from it and begin to move forward as you Let Go and Let God!*

I am a firm believer that God puts people in every part of our lives to help us get through whatever we might be facing. Whether it is to encourage us, protect us, shelter us, or just be a role model to us. We are all God's good Samaritans to some effect....at least when we heed the calling. What is resonant about the request to participate in this project is the fact that I received it on Mother's Day, which is how I met Jamicka. I was introduced to Mrs. Jones through a mutual friend for whom I was pregnant. I don't know if Mrs. Jones knew of the complications we had created or the ripple effect of consequences both of her friends would have to face because of their union, but she welcomed us into her home and into her life. You see, at the time, I was struggling with the thought of being a mother. How would it affect my life and the people around me? Would it hinder me from accomplishing my goals? Would my family look at me with shame in their eyes? Would I be able to raise her on my own or would I have to depend on my mother to look after "her" while I was deployed or away?

I didn't know this then and was blinded by my fear of uncertainty, but God was showing me the answers to my questions through Jamicka. You see, as we became closer friends, Jamicka shared with me the history of her life in the military, her marriage to her husband, her love for her kids and family, and her passions in life. One day she allowed me the chance to babysit her boys-J'Don, and Jamal. As nerve wrecking as it was, it was also very rewarding. It showed me that I might not have all the answers but if you just tried your best everything else would fall into place. It was my AHA moment or at least the moment where I felt strong enough to call my mom to tell her the news.

The call home was something I neither expected nor could have prepared for. Upon my cordials and greetings, my Mom started sobbing and explaining to me that my brother was imprisoned for accidentally killing someone. I immediately froze. My tears of sorrow for my brother and the guy that lost his life muffled my news of the pregnancy. I was infused with fear once again, and the questions came back. However, this time it was more about shame than my capabilities. Yes, a child is a blessing but I didn't think so or know how much of a blessing they could be at the time. I didn't know how my child could turn out to be good when it was formed in such a complicated way. It was never the pregnancy which was complicated but the fact that I was pregnant out of wedlock, pregnant at 21 with no degree or idea of where I was going, and pregnant by a married man. All of this going against the morals and values I was taught in a Christian home.

My fears made me run, and needless to say I tried to cover up my situation by opting to have an abortion. Although I have owned up to my decision to abort, I have suffered with depression and regret of it for awhile. However, Mrs. Jones has been my Good Samaritan. She has helped me out when I was down and taught me to let people in as I am. She has taught me that God didn't call us to be perfect but He called us to be a blessing to others and share His word. I ran from shame and fumbled my faith and through searching for her I found strength….strength to answer when He calls no matter the challenge. **You Matter** no matter your background!

All the best with your book Jamicka, Thank you for letting me be a part of your life and this incredible journey. Forgive me for writing so much but this is actually a healing moment and testimony for me.

CC Smiles- Iraq

# CHAPTER SEVENTEEN
# A MARRIAGE MIRACLE

*If you don't have a #1 fan ... you can't have mine! This lady is always there to cheer you on whether in person, via social media, email, phone call, or text. Sometimes you have to push others to help them get through. Don't stop pushing and never give up!*

Jamicka Louise Jones, that's what I learned your name was and would lovingly call you. You are one of my dearest and closest friends! I cannot tell you the day, month, or year we met. I can tell you it was a colder month in Spanaway, WA at Lively Hope COGIC Church. I remember that because I remember admiring the casual hat and long skirt you were wearing. You were so nicely and casually put together. I was immediately drawn to your friendly personality and welcoming spirit. I was some 3,000 miles away from my family in NC and felt so alone. I needed you, right then, right there. That was truly a God-designed meeting.

Although I didn't know the plans God had for me, for good and not of evil, to give me a future and a hope, Jeremiah 29:11, I did recognize He was using you to bless me. Very quickly, I found myself feeling comfortable enough to be completely transparent--my marriage was falling apart. I now know the reason I felt safe to share with you very intimate details of my failing marriage. It was God's love in you that caused you to love me deeply and allowed me to feel forgiven for my wrongs, 1Peter 4:8. It was the single most miraculous memory, one I will always cherish--your contagious faith! Do you remember? Do you remember what I would always say to you?

"Thank you for believing...thank you for believing when I didn't!" You believed God would save my marriage when I doubted. You never got tired of listening to me cry it out. Your faith was so amazingly powerful, I believed because you did, "Janice, God's gonna do it; He's already done it!" You were so right! To God be the glory!

Our spiritual bond grew stronger and stronger over time, and a life-long friendship developed that has withstood the test of time and Uncle Sam's Army. Before making the east coast my home again, we created lasting memories: celebrated J'Don and Jamal's birthday parties (whose themes you created, cakes you baked, pictures you took, and activities you crafted), shared in the holidays, and worshiped our Lord together, just a few of so, so many. I even shared in the birth of your last bundle of joy, Absalom, just like I was there. Your thoughtfulness never forgets to include those dearest to you. You are a virtuous, powerful woman of God, and your fortitude is so inspiring: You entered the Mrs. WA pageant and won Mrs. Congeniality, went back to school after (I forgot how long-friends are allowed, right? =) and earned your Bachelor's Degree, licensed to own a photography business, and achieved a childhood dream to deliver a public motivational speech. In addition to these accomplishments, (I didn't even name them all), you kept (still do) yourself healthy and beautiful, with nutritional eating choices and regular fitness activities, such as biking and Zumba (I think you got addicted).

I could go on, but I'll save room for someone else. Jamicka Louise Jones, I love you! I am honored and count it a blessing to say, "You are my friend, and I am your friend!" Therefore [let us] encourage one another and build one another up, just as you are doing. ~ I Thessalonians 5:11~

Janice Gordon- Fort Drum, NY

# CHAPTER EIGHTEEN
# USR REPORTS TURNED FRIENDSHIP

*If you've ever seen the movie, "A Christmas Story", then you know the scene of eating at a Chinese Restaurant on Christmas Day. Our families did that together one year. Although not planned, it was one of the most memorable Christmas' for both of our families.*

As a newly commissioned US Army Officer assigned to Joint Base Lewis Mc Chord I was eager to excel at my job. I was always on the hunt for any information that could serve to increase my knowledge or mentoring and leadership opportunities to provide me with the valuable experience I was lacking. While working on a project for my unit that I was a little unsure of how to accomplish I had to meet with one of the Civilian Government Employees on base. The woman that I was originally scheduled to meet with was preoccupied. Thankfully, a young lady by the name of Jamicka Jones offered me assistance.

One of the first things I noticed about her was the pictures of her children, two vibrant boys and her husband, in addition to a flyer from a church for an event. The combination of her cordiality and the fact that I was on the hunt for a church made me inquire about where she attended services. Forty minutes later we had exchanged information about our respective families and I had a standing invitation to her church. If that weren't enough, I not only completed my task but Jamicka had also taught me how to complete it in a much timelier and effective manner for the next time.

Jamicka could have not assisted me and taken a break at a job that provided few. She wouldn't of been wrong since my unit was not one that she was assigned to support. But that isn't Jamicka. She sees a person in need and despite how fatigued she may be she still helps those who need it. She could have chosen not to discuss her family or church, often times taboo subjects with those that you don't know. She would have been well within her rights but seeing that I was new and in search of a spiritual home she assisted.

Her family and mine have a friendship that has endured distance and time. They are the quintessential American Family whose foundation is built in their spiritual faith, love of family, and community. The American ideals of discipline, respect, and hard work are present in abundance in the Jones family.

Seven years later I think of the friendship she and my wife share, I and her husband share, her sons and mine share and couldn't imagine what life would be like without their presence in our lives. We have vacationed together, shared holidays together, and supported each other through good times and bad. Through it all she has always made time for us despite how tired she may be, opened the doors to her home without hesitation and provided my family with a friendship that has always been unconditional. That is who Jamicka Jones is.

While it's true that there are no shortage of self-help and how to books on the market, every so often you find a diamond in the ruff.

There are rare times when a literary work is produced with the primary intention of improving the lives of others more so than their own fortune.

Jamicka Jones is just the type of selfless individual to write a book that shares experiences that enlighten and enrich the soul of the reader. Her words inspire without making her achievements appear unattainable, and encourage without preaching or being condescending.

Jamicka strikes a perfect balance between hardships and triumphs and weaves snapshots of her life into a heartwarming book that provides lessons that cross gender and racial boundaries. It's the type of book that you will get something out of, that can be read multiple times and will still offer something new to the reader every time. Having personally viewed her and her family achieve successes and overcome obstacles I can attest to her perseverance and sincere desire to help others.

CPT Ori Avila – US Army   Aberdeen Proving Grounds, MD

# CHAPTER NINETEEN
# A GOAL FULFILLED AT A CHRISTIAN UNIVERSITY

*"Finish the Race, Complete the Work, Get the Job Done" — the Most Valuable Motivator (MVM) - James Edwards*

When I hear people talk about friends or see a TV show or movie including fun scenes among them, I can't help but think of my very closest friends who are so close they are like my sisters. And one of them is my dear friend Jamicka Jones. We met while attending college at Northwest University. We have managed to keep in touch since graduation and although we do not see or speak to each other every day, we pick up like it was just yesterday when we do reconnect.

Back to our college days, Jamicka and I first met when we were in Biblical Exegesis. The funny thing is that at the time both of us were going through extreme stress and were just thankful to have made it into the class. She still remembers me giving her a business card with a flower image and my favorite bible verse, I Corinthians 13:13 - "And now these three remain: faith, hope and love. But the greatest of these is love." I was amazed the other day when she said she remembered that about our first meeting and that because of my genuine friendliness she knew I'd be a friend for life. That brings a smile to my face and joy to my heart. And the thing is, I remember feeling at home with her too. I knew she was a special kind of person, one you don't meet every day and knowing her would bring something extra to my life.

Something I really appreciate about her is that I can always count on her to see a point of view that I have overlooked and see the optimism in even the most negative of situations. To have those great qualities and the characteristic of being a loyal friend through it all is like having wonderful blessings all rolled into one big blessing in a dear friend. Jamicka has always taken the time to help me out, even when I just needed to hear her voice or read a message from her that would help me see the light at the end of whatever tunnel in which I have found myself stuck.

I admire this woman, who I am so lucky to call a friend because she overcame hurdles that could have potentially prevented her from accomplishing her goals.

While we were in our Undergrad Program, she remained a loving and caring wife and mother, was selected to be part of an elite group of African American college students featured in a calendar, and even reigned as Mrs. Fife and was elected by her pageant peers as Mrs. Congeniality by the way.

If you met her, you would know why she was chosen because you would absolutely recognize her vibrant energy and it is contagious. Yes, she did this while we made our way through our university days which was not easy. To top it off, she planned a celebration cruise for all the lovely women in her life to attend which was like the icing on the cake after graduation. And this wonderful friend is doing something I have wanted to do for a very long time, she is writing a book. Once again, I am motivated by her pursuit of a goal and am still very proud to be able to call her my friend.

A true friend will be by your side, even if they cannot be there literally. You can tell her anything and she will not judge you but will keep your best interests in mind and be that support you need to help you through. And as her friend, you would do the same in return. You don't keep track of who helped who last or who contacted who last. We know we have busy lives but we also know our lives would not be the same without each other.

Our becoming friend was a blessing, "it was God" as we have said when we realize many things that have happened over the years. And in this type of true friendship, you experience love. I love my dear friend and always want the best for her and her family. It is just like the bible verse says...."the greatest of these is love"....love your family and friends because they are God's blessings in our lives....love you Jamicka! Thank you for being a very good friend!!!!
:)  With Love & Friendship ~

Neclisa - Northwest University- Kirkland, WA Classmate & Graduate 2010

## CHAPTER TWENTY
## REAL LIFE, REAL PEOPLE, REAL LOVE-
## INTEGRITY LIFE CHURCH (ILC)

*I'll never forget my first friend at ILC- someone who barely knew me, but came to support me as I ran for Mrs. Washington America. She believed in me and I believe in her. Never forget those who support you when they know nothing about you!*

Jamicka Jones is one of the greatest women I've met in my life. She's real, tough, kind, honest, integral, always giving of herself to help someone, and just an all-around great person.

I can remember seeing her big bright smile at church one Sunday and right in that moment she came, said hello, and handed me an invitation to her Mrs. Fife gathering. I thanked her and she hugged me with sincerity. I can recall thinking, "she seems like the real deal kind of person I miss from back home." See I'm from Massachusetts and I'm used to a little more warmth from people than I've experienced here I'm Washington state. Because of her bright smile and sincere hug, I knew I was going to go support her event.

As I walked in the door the night of the event, there was that genuine smile again. Greeting her guests and just simply being herself. It was a fun night, great turnout, and I just remember seeing her be the exact same smiley, loving person with everyone.

Jamicka and I connected from there. Not hanging out all the time, not even visiting each other's homes often or anything. It was just a real heart connection. We'd have what I call, quick chats (but meaningful) about family, her boys' activities and sports, work, her schooling, marriage (she so wanted me to get married because she knew my heart's desire), etc. She met my daughter, I met her husband and at that time, her two boys. We kept in touch with a handful of phone calls, lots of hugs and laughter after church, text messages, and a few visits from time to time.

One major topic of a few of our conversations was her love for photography. We would be in church and she always had a camera. You'd turn around and she was snapping pictures and smiling, catching us all in the perfect unexpected shots.

When I asked her if she'd take some Three Generation pictures for me, I remember hearing her smile over the phone. She was so humbled, yet very honored, that I would ask her. We scheduled the appointment, and she did an awesome job. I believe we were part of her first few "real customers" as she says, maybe even the very first.

Then came a season of challenge and change for the Jones's. With her pregnancy and birth of baby boy #3, Jamicka had to slow down in a very real way. The very active and involved wife/mom couldn't move around as usual and they needed some help. I never told her this, but even the way she asked for help was touching to me. She was so open, unashamed, and real about their situation, and I honor that in people. Needless to say, I knew I would do whatever I could to step right in.

Throughout that tough season, one thing remained unchanged. Jamicka's smile, sincerity, and strength superseded all else. What a blessing to witness and take part in. My help involved me coming over more than usual and, again, something I never shared, the entire family inspired me and made me smile on the inside as I was helping them. I was in a tough season myself and they brightened my days.

I'm so very grateful for my friend Mrs. Jamicka Jones. We don't see each other often, and talk even less than that but one thing is for certain. Our hearts are forever connected, we are there for each other right when we're needed, and I thank God for our friendship that is indeed for life.

Courtney Jenkins- Tacoma, WA

# CHAPTER TWENTY-ONE
# BEEHIVE BOOKSTORE

*It was the first summer after homeschooling our sons and I needed a mini break.
I dropped them off at a Vacation Bible School and accidentally found this cute
bookstore that I just couldn't resist the urge to go inside.*

Each day at our small-town Christian bookstore, in a rural suburb of Seattle, is an adventure. Friends and strangers walk through the door, all in-search of some type of inspiration, healing, or hope. Maybe it was Spring-time when Jamicka walked into the bookstore, nearly six years ago. It could have been gloomy and raining outside, but Jamicka's smile and countenance made it seem like a fresh, sunny spring day. We began talking, first as strangers -- bookstore owner and potential customer. It didn't take long to get past the chit-chat of first meetings as our conversation melted into deeper matters of the heart. We talked about the goodness of God and the importance of marriage and families. We parted with a hug and a smile, like old-time friends.

Since that day years ago, our paths have crossed a dozen times or so. We text or e-mail each other, seemingly just at the right moment. I remember a spontaneous visit when Jamicka came to our home with her boys, but not as her usual bubbly, happy self. She came for help and advice. Freshly baked bread was just out of the oven. We enjoyed some comfort food and comforting words. Hours later, I watched her and her sleeping boys wrapped in blankets, leave into the dark and drive away. She left a stronger woman . . . and left me with more admiration for her courage and fortitude.

A year or so later, I visited Jamicka in the hospital while she was bed-ridden with her last pregnancy. We visited and giggled. I was there to uplift her, but I left feeling uplifted.

My life has been enriched and enlarged by meeting this woman who just happened to stop by a little bookstore, with a few moments to spare. Call our meeting coincidence, but I think it's more than that. I call it divine intervention.

Chrissy Cope- Milton, WA

# CHAPTER TWENTY-TWO
# COLLEGE CHURCH GIRL

*A young, but mature lady caught my attention and I had to get to know her better!*

The year I met Jamicka Jones was 2009. I had just graduated from college and joined a new church, where Jamicka was already a member. We were connected through the Pastors of the church. They mentioned how I was a recent graduate, and how they were happy that I was there. Jamicka was the youth activities coordinator at that time for the church. She put together outings and facilitated events at the church.

She was always really nice and said hello when we saw each other and one day she asked me about being a chaperone with the youth for an educational event that she had set up. She was just about the first person at the church to truly embrace me into their ministry. I agreed, and throughout the outing she and I began to talk more as we were watching the youth. She truly took an interest in what I was doing in life and we began to talk more.

This experience was truly special because being a young college graduate starting at a new church where you don't really know anyone, and then to have someone come up and truly take an interest in you as a person and as an asset to truly help was wonderful. At the time that I had joined there weren't too many people my age at the church and though Jamicka was not my age she was still very much youthful and lively and it was nice to bounce ideas and listen to her experiences.

It was truly amazing that she allowed her love for God and her ministry to show through and reach me. To this day she and I are not in constant contact, but she is the same person now as she was almost 5 years ago, and I can still talk to her and learn from her to this day.

Lachelle of Kent, WA

## CHAPTER TWENTY-THREE
## LONG LOST COUSIN

*It's never too late to get to know your family. Do you have the time?*

Jamicka Jones, is a powerful, impactful, passionate, loving, humble, sympathetic, emphatic, wonderful, amazing and caring woman..

Jamicka is my cousin and I love and respect her. She talks the talk and walks the walk.. She is a proven and trustworthy leader. She and I grew up worlds apart but uphold the same life principles and standards. Our communications with one another came later in our lives and I will say in these past few years she has ignited a fire in me that I allowed to burn out.

I too am a motivator, but I put my gift on a shelf to collect dust. Our conversations we shared, seeing the impact that she is making in the community, and around the country reminded me of my destiny. She constantly reminds me that my gift is not for me but to the world. I thank God for her and I pray that the Lord elevates her beyond her vision and imagination. Thank you, Jamicka, for keeping your beacon of light shining. You are an angel sent from heaven to spread the good news. I love you. –

Phillip Barr – Belleville, IL

## CHAPTER TWENTY-FOUR
## ZUMBA FEVER!!!!

*I love to Zumba and in a Zumba class; people know how much I love it! This lady enjoyed my energy and I enjoyed her.*

About a year ago my gym discontinued Friday night Zumba so I started to go to the Saturday morning class and beside me every week was this friendly, fun-loving young woman named Jamicka, whose energy was very contagious. Due to her whole-hearted involvement, my workouts were not only fun, but my level of participation was increased both physically and verbally!

Injuries have kept me away from the gym for months now, but Jamicka and I have stayed in touch texting and occasionally she even finds the time out of her busy schedule to meet for coffee or frozen yogurt. It is a pleasure to visit with her. She is thoughtful, always has a positive outlook, and so often shares kind words and encouragement.

I don't know exactly when she gave her first motivational speech, but when she e-mailed it for me to view, she had no idea the timing was perfect. It was only October, but I had just purchased a desktop calendar with daily inspirations for the coming year, and had already opened it up to start reading them in order to gain some motivation, determination, and inspiration - the things that Jamicka also delivered in her speech.

In January 2014, I had the privilege of attending a Martin Luther King assembly that Jamicka planned, organized, and led the students at her high school where she currently works. I was impressed with the wonderful job she did of both the planning and the presentation. Jamicka is definitely a leader who is setting a great example, not only for her boys, but for all the kids that are lucky enough to have her working at their school!

Cindy Reichman- Lakewood, WA

# CHAPTER TWENTY-FIVE
# JENSEN GYM MEETING

*Sometimes you've been hurt in past friendships and it's hard to allow new friendships to evolve. The day we met we both had a wall up but something told us to connect. Can't imagine if we hadn't..... you will feel the same way after reading this story. Sometimes you have to open your heart for new friendships, new relationships.*

I'll never forget the day I met Jamicka. I remember waking up one morning in my cold, empty house after returning from a long flight the night before. I spent the few days prior driving with my husband out of state after his new job position relocated him. We said it would be a quick nine months apart, and I told him to take all the furniture with him (minus the futon, a television, and some kitchen supplies) since I didn't want to worry about it when it was time for me to join him. Our first morning apart was New Year's Eve 2012. I was sad and on the brink of tears. The thought of ringing in 2013 in that sad emotional state was so unappealing to me. I knew I had to shake it off somehow. I've always been into fitness, so what better way to start the New Year off right than with a good workout.

Heading to the gym on post, my spirits immediately lifted. I knew this was the best "medicine" for me to help me move past the loneliness of my best friend being nearly 2,000 miles away from me. I decided to try something different, Zumba. The class was high energy, fun, and addictive. I knew I'd want to come back. On my way to walk out of the class, a young exuberant woman with bright eyes by the name of Jamicka Jones approached me and asked if I'd been to the class before. I told her it was my first Zumba experience. We kept talking all the way to the parking lot. Come to find out we had the same recent weight loss experience. Having the same excitement for fitness in common was definitely a common denominator. We exchanged phone numbers and promised to keep in touch. Sadly, I walked away not expecting to ever hear from her again. Meeting people seems so difficult the older I get, and I've been bamboozled by the "let's do lunch" and the "I'll call you sometime" some-timey people that I didn't expect to hear from her.

Much to my amazement, Jamicka not only kept her word with sending me text messages throughout the next week, but we also planned to meet up at more of the aerobics classes on post. What became an unexpected friendship, soon blossomed into us running in a community wide run on her birthday of all days, to sushi outings (we quickly came to see that we have a love for food in common...), and my spending time with her family for weekend home cooked meals.

I often asked God why did he allow someone so kind hearted and so much like me to come into my life just before my relocation from the area nine months after meeting her. He reminds me every day that our friendship is not seasonal or "reasonal", but instead it's one for a lifetime. She is my sister through and through. She is the most unconditionally loving person I know. She possesses a degree of understanding and patience that I wish most people would emulate.

I was sad to say goodbye to her the day I finally left Washington State. We reminded each other, "It's not goodbye, but rather see-you-soon." We've kept in touch over the months with such ease. We have a friendship in which you can fully be yourself, without punishment for sharing an unpopular opinion, and where you don't feel that keeping in touch is an obligation but rather a blessing. I can say with certainty that she is such a special part of this world and to other people. She has a knack for touching your life at just the right time. God knew what he was doing December 31, 2012, and I am forever grateful!

Lacia- Nebraska

# CHAPTER TWENTY-SIX
## My WAEOP MOTHER- Washington Association of Educational Office Professionals

*How can I have an 80 plus year old friend that truly adores me and can teach, nurture, and provide so much wisdom and yet treat me as if I'm a great friend she's had for years. This is how…..*

My first sight and welcome to Jamicka was in Richland, Washington at the WAEOP Spring conference, April 26, 2013. She was a breath of fresh air, with so much exuberance and enthusiasm. I was especially impressed with her sincere and genuine interest in WAEOP and NAEOP. So many times, new members are reluctant to get involved but not Jamicka. She entered into discussions, had excellent questions and got so much out of the conference. She was nominated and placed on our election ballot as an Area Director for the State of Washington. She was elected to the 2-year term and I had the pleasure of installing her on the board April 26, 2014. I would say Jamicka made great strides in one year.

I was enthusiastic when I first joined WAEOP in 1958, but small children, a busy teacher-coach for a husband, and limited finances kept me from getting too involved. It took me fifteen years to go to my first National (NAEOP) conference and Jamicka attended her first national conference in 2013 still in her first year of membership. Really an amazing lady! She applied for her PSP- Performance Standard Program & CEOE- Certified Educational Office Employee certifications as early as she was eligible. These are more amazing accomplishments. All of this sums up what an impression Jamicka has had on me. She renews my spirit, my belief in WAEOP and my love for our organization. It gives me faith in our future: with Jamicka we are in good hands.

Paula Thomas- Naches, WA


*Paula Thomas has been a WAEOP Member for over 50 years. She is truly a gem and a woman of great wisdom with a beautiful heart and spirit. I am so blessed to have gotten to know her and can say she is truly one of my friends.*

# CHAPTER TWENTY-SEVEN
# NEW POSITION, NEW TRAINING, NEW FRIEND

*Be who you are at all times, you never know who's watching you and what you may be doing for them.*

My name is Rhonda Quinton and I met Jamicka Jones at the Washington Association of Educational Office Professionals (WAEOP) Spring Conference in Richland, Washington in April of 2013. Although I don't know her very well yet, my first impressions of her were: she was energetic, friendly, she's a go getter, has a great listening ear, and has goals she has met and continues to meet.

Jamicka and I, had both signed up for the same class and that was how I first met her. In this class, Jamicka asked several questions and shared some of her present experiences in a new job position she had just started. Jamicka was eager to hear what others in the class had to say about similar things that might be happening in their schools and any steps they used that would be helpful for her in her new position. She took notes of the different things that would be useful to her in her new position and seemed excited to go back to her supervisor at school and report.

Jamicka is a fun spirited person to be around and I really enjoy that about her. The times that I have been around her, she has been upbeat, has had a positive attitude and she is not afraid to step up and try something new or take on new challenges.

Jamicka is dedicated and determined to reach any goals that she set for herself. I consider Jamicka a friend and I wish her success in all things.

Thank you for this opportunity for me to share some thoughts about Jamicka and I truly wish her all the best!!

Sincerely,

Rhonda Quinton- WA

# CHAPTER TWENTY-EIGHT
# MARRIOTT- VA

*Sometimes being at the wrong place at the right time is just how God wants it. Don't get flustered the next time your plans don't go exactly right, or if you get lost or if you arrive at the wrong location. …You just may make a new friend in the process.*

As the adage goes, "all things happen for a reason." I'm not sure about all things however, I am certain that my encounter with Jamicka Jones was nothing less than of the divine.

With my hair flying in every coordinate possible, lugging my belongings about, and hoping that I could get to my room in a timely manner, while not finding a lunch that only Trump could afford; to my left stood this bright spirited young lady. How was she so calm? The hustle of travel did not induce a virtual myocardial infarction! She was radiant and clear minded. She was Jamicka. Her friendly eyes met mine and literally made me forget about all of the hustle and bustle.

We engaged in small talk and then shared the reason for our travel to the District of Columbia. She was slated to attend a remarkable conference, while I was slated to volunteer with an international youth mentoring program. Plus, I lived in the District for years. So it was good to be back in the old proverbial stomping ground.

Jamicka and I became friends immediately. We shared more about our current careers and life goals. Interestingly, we shared much in common. I am a scientist and have been signed as a professional public speaker. I promise that both tasks are extremely exciting. Don't hate on science. Geek is chic! The motivational speaking really broke ground and introduced loads of conversation.

I remember Jamicka stating that I inspired her. To this day, I have no clue how. We simply talked and connected. Maybe therein lies the magic. Connections inspire. There was something unique about her zeal for life and zest to plant seeds of goodness into each person she encountered. It was highly evident that she lived life deliberately. That simple observation pleasantly reminds me of the power in being deliberate and focused.

As fate would have it, I was on the wrong shuttle bus! However, my encounter with Jamicka was well worth the mix up. As shared in the introduction, some things carry a spark of the divine and are sincerely destined to happen.

When you feel that hint of destiny, what do you do? Do you continue mindlessly, muddling about your hurry and over-committed schedule? Or, do you follow that gentle prodding to connect. In this grand universe, we are all connected regardless of race, creed, gender, religion, or fashion sense.

Let us remember to deliberately reach out and get connected. The power is remarkable. True connections are simply sensational. Take time to connect. Make time to inspire.

Joy Obidike

## CHAPTER TWENTY-NINE
## SPEAKERS BUREAU CLASSMATE

*First impressions are not always lasting impressions.*

So, I'm sitting in this hotel classroom in July, 2013, waiting in great anticipation for the class to begin. This is the very first - virgin voyage - greatest opportunity of my life to learn how to become a public speaker. Before coming to the conference, our instructors had emailed us an assignment. I had completed my assignment! I sat on the edge of my chair ready to take in every word of instruction. I felt inspired and privileged to be part of this test-run class. Because of my slightly English heritage and my "listen-to-your-elders upbringing", I arrived early, of course, and sat upright in my chair. I came prepared, eager to learn, and ready to take it all in. I remember my excitement when one of the four instructors closed the door and introduced herself. Alright, we're ready to begin learning how to be the best public speaker in the world.

Class had only been underway for a few minutes, when one of the gals sitting behind me, received a phone call. REALLY!!!??? How could she open herself up to distractions? Doesn't she know this is the opportunity of a life time to concentrate on ourselves? She bopped out of class to take the call and returned a few minutes later. I remember her "bopping" in and out of class a couple more times over the two day course of instruction.

It wasn't my business to ask her to just sit still and take in all of the elite education we were receiving. It wasn't my business at all. I focused my attention on the educational parade performing in front of me.

When each of us was asked to introduce ourselves, I learned this ball of energy was Jamicka Jones. Of course, her name is Jamicka Jones. That name rolls off your tongue like a bouncing ball. I thought, "Her name suits her well." She has energy pouring out of every pore of her skin. Throughout the two day Speakers' Bureau, I learned that Jamicka is a loving wife, mother of a number of children, active in many school, church and community events. When it was Jamicka's opportunity to present to our class, I saw her tender caring heart and her deep desire to become a public speaker. I was convinced that Jamicka would pass this class with the skills necessary to reach the world with her ability to bring joy and inspiration to any group she chose to speak to.

Months after we "graduated" from the Speakers Bureau, I received a video of Jamicka's public "bucket" presentation. She made me smile seeing her walk into a crowded room of children and adults and balanced on both sides of her body were buckets on each of her arms. I was excited for Jamicka and for those who heard her speak. Jamicka Jones speaks to people from her heart. Her heart touched me that day in our class with the words she spoke, with the tears she cried, with the determined joy she was finding in life.

I won't forget Jamicka Jones. Meeting Jamicka and spending two days in class with her, reminded me that though we are wrapped in different bodies and experienced different ways of being raised, our hearts are on identical paths, with the deep desire to reach people with new ideas, anxious to impart to others an awareness of the strength that lies within their reach, determined to help others realize their potential and live out their dreams.

Sylvia S. Sullivan,

Resides in Wagener, South Carolina; and lives with one foot in Heaven

# CHAPTER THIRTY
# SHOE BLESSINGS

*Sometimes hear a person speak in a non-church setting and you want to say
AMEN to everything they say. This is what happened when I first heard this
lady speak in a class. So blessed to call her my friend today.*

On a beautiful day July 2013, in Alexandria, VA, I met a most
precious and beautiful young woman named Jamicka Jones, from the
state of Washington. Such a bright and warm spirit from what I
experienced as a wet and dreary state. I attended my first National
NAEOP Conference in Seattle, Washington some years ago. It
rained for the entire week, my flight was delayed, I arrived in the wee
hours of the morning to a strange airport in a new city all alone and I
was not on the registration list. What a trip to a place I vowed, I
would not visit again. However, after meeting this sweet,
sweet Jamicka Jones, who adds a bright spot to the state of
Washington, I have decided that I will visit again just to see her and
meet her handsome family.

Jamicka and I were in a class together. We were two of the first
participants of the NAEOP Alley Faye "Facilitators Training Class".
We became instant friends, because, I don't believe Jamicka comes
into contact with anyone who is not a friend. To see her makes you
smile and to know her changes your life. She is always positive and
she is just a genuine person.

Over the two days of all day training, the conversations that took us from being acquainted to friends was the day I complimented her high heel tan pumps. You see Jamicka has a very stylish and classy image and on this particular day, she would be making her presentation to the class, so the high heels and nicely tied scarf around her neck, really made her stand out. I noticed the high heels because I can no longer wear more than a 2" heel. I told her how jealous I was of her high heels and we laughed.

Jamicka shared with me that her husband had bought her those shoes for the conference and that she did not have a lot of shoes. She and her husband was a happily married young couple with three handsome young sons. Jamicka said that she knew how to stretch a dollar to maintain their household budget. We talked at lunch and at every break. On the last day of our training, I asked her what size shoe she wore and she responded a size 7. I promised Jamicka a surprise and asked for her home address. A few weeks or maybe a month or so later, I kept my promise and sent a large box to the state of Washington. It still gives me great joy to have been able to be a blessing to such a blessed woman.

Jamicka is so unique that for Christmas, she took the time to hand write a letter to me detailing her family's year and she also sent me a family picture. In this day of technology, receiving that letter was very dear to me and so is Mrs. Jamicka Jones.

To have a friend, you must first be a friend. Thank you for being my friend! All the best to you in the future. I know that you will be tied to GREAT THINGS!

Love you to life,

Robyn Bumbry

# CHAPTER THIRTY-ONE
# STUDENT TEACHING TO FULL-TIME TEACHER

*Passing through the office by happenstance leads to everlasting friendship by choice.*

My very first encounter with Jamicka was actually a humorous misunderstanding. I was student teaching at Steilacoom High School and on that particular day I was leading mock job interviews for the students so everyone was dressed in professional wear. Being only 22, I still looked like I could be in high school, especially in a room full of well-dressed teenagers. Jamicka walked into my classroom with an adult volunteer for the interviews and was trying to direct the lady to the "teacher" for further instruction. Jamicka came up to me, thinking I was just another student, and asked me where one of the teachers was. Not knowing that she was actually looking for me I directed her to the teacher she was looking for. A few minutes later Jamicka came back laughing as she realized she had been searching for me all along.

Since then my friendship with Jamicka has blossomed very quickly in just a few short months. I told Jamicka that I would be getting married in July and she mentioned to me that she was a photographer. As fate would have it, I was actually looking for someone to take our engagement pictures. So on a freezing December day out by the water Jamicka braved the cold, got to meet my fiancé, and took some gorgeous photos for us. Now that I don't work at Steilacoom High School anymore I miss being able to walk by Jamicka's office to say hi every day. But we still keep in touch often as she will be the photographer for my wedding day as well.

Getting to know Jamicka these last few months has been extremely inspirational. She has shared with me her dreams as a mother, wife, photographer, motivational speaker, bookkeeper, community activist, hair stylist, make-up artist, and now author. It seems like there is nothing Jamicka can't do and I so admire her for her dedication and drive to living a fulfilling life. I am so appreciative of that humorous misunderstanding that very first day for it has turned into an incredible friendship.

Lori Emery- Lakewood, WA

# CHAPTER THIRTY-TWO
# VENDOR TURNED FRIENDSHIP

*A supportive friendship connected through business.*

I own a very successful company which provides products at the location Jamicka Jones currently works. I have had the privilege of knowing and working with Jamicka for six months. I am thoroughly impressed by her and what she represents, which is hard work, dedication, and diligence in getting the job done.

It is not the loyalty of her job responsibilities that stand out to me; it is the human attributes she displays. The vibrant, enthusiastic, contagious personality does nothing but uplift those in her presence. Her face continuously has that welcome smile and people gravitate to her like metal to a magnet. I embrace my friendship with Jamicka.

She has enlightened me and brought a spark in my life because of her great spirit. I hope whoever reads this has the opportunity to meet and get to know this extraordinary woman. You would be happy and pleased that you did.

Larry Olson- Rainier Apparel Owner/President – Steilacoom, WA

# CHAPTER THIRTY-THREE
# TECHNICAL COMPATIBILITIES

*Every day, I look forward to and get excited about who God is going to connect me with next. This lady was so helpful, calm, and sweet. When we met, her spirit was amazing and it was exactly what I needed in preparing for one of the biggest moments in my life.*

My name is Maybeline Jenkins; I'm an office coordinator for a Tacoma Public Schools, Professional Development Center (PDC). Jamicka was the guest speaker at the FCCLA event that took place at the PDC on October 17, 2013.

Many people come and go throughout our lives. We may meet a person at a store, on a walk, or at your place of work and that person may stay with us as a friend, or leave us like it's an end of a small era. I have met many people in my line of work; sometimes I meet a few who really touch or edify me in a big way. Jamicka is one of those people. I was making my morning rounds checking the rooms to ensure all equipment was up and running for my customers. I walked into one of the meeting rooms and there she was preparing for one of her workshops that day, looking superb. Right away I felt kinship as the connection was so strong. She shared with me this was her first official keynote speaking engagement to a big audience. It was taking place later that day. Also, this was one of her dreams that has finally manifested. Since the kinship was so strong, I decided that I would come down and listen to her speak.

Let me summarize in my own words, something short of what I heard from Jamicka's testimony. Follow your passion and live your purpose. "If you have the passion to do something, then you also have the power to make it happen. She had hit a lot of obstacles, but with the Lord she was conquering and even more determined to seek her passion to encourage the ones that the world believes are losers. While she always remembers the positive people who told her she could accomplish something, she cherishes and holds a special place in her heart for her encouragers. So often the difference between success and failure is belief and so often that belief is instilled in us by someone who encouraged us.

Today Jamicka's passion is to encourage others and be that person who instills a positive belief in someone who needs to hear her encouraging words. Uplift someone who is feeling down and second best with her fuel of positive energy.

Rallying others to focus on what is possible rather than what seems impossible. I left that meeting with tears in my eyes. I am encouraged once again! The world needs more people to speak into the hearts of others and say "I believe in you."

Maybeline Jenkins- Tacoma, WA

# CHAPTER THIRTY-FOUR
# CHANCE ENCOUNTER

*You're tired after a long day, know you have things to do, but just when you're getting a late night cup of coffee you see a new friend you made earlier that day. Do you stop and say "Hi" or keep going? Well, I chose to say "Hi" and two hours later….*

In the fall of 2013 I went to Moses Lake for a weekend of learning, laughter and fun with Educational Office Professionals from across the state of Washington. The theme for our weekend was "Never Ending Training" which piqued my curiosity even though I am retired from my job as an Education Office Professional. I met an energetic young woman who blessed me in so many ways. One evening in the hotel lobby, where I was reading a book, I saw Jamicka who I had met earlier in the day, and said 'hello'. That led to nearly two hours of late night conversation and sharing. She had planned to use this weekend away from her family to not only grow professionally and refresh herself to return to her job and family rested and energized, but also to prepare a motivational presentation which she was to give to high school students the next Thursday!

Jamicka has high expectations for herself as a mom, wife and being the best person God wants her to be. Serving in the military has taught her discipline, allowed her to grow personally and has given her a strong sense of self-worth. Eventually our conversation became personal and we talked of our faith and the love we have for our Lord, a profound common bond we share. Our faith journeys have taken us places and through situations we never imagined only to become better people because of them. Without faith and prayer, day to day living can become monotonous. Meeting Jamicka, and sharing with her, definitely encouraged me in my faith journey and reminded me that living with God is definitely not monotonous.

Relationships are built on those encounters we have with people whether for a moment, a day or a lifetime. I sincerely believe this to be true. Thank you, Jamicka Jones, for sharing those precious moments with me, moments I'll not forget.

God Bless you,
Janice Stepp- Shoreline, WA

# CHAPTER THIRTY-FIVE
# WHAT GOD SAYS ABOUT YOU <u>MATTERS</u>, NO MATTER WHEN HE SAID IT!

*My campaign manager for the Crown of Mrs. Washington America 2009.*

In the beginning of starting out at my 6<sup>th</sup> College, there was a very unique student in one of my classes. His name was Hal Raines. In my first class with him, he was always so quiet and shy. He didn't say much, but when he spoke or asked the professor a question you listened. During our breaks, sometimes, Hal and I would talk about church and different things. Through our conversations, I discovered his true gift and talent was working behind a camera. He enjoyed filming anything from church services, special events, and music videos. I also learned that he was very tech savvy and he had some mad DJ skills. After our semester was over, Hal told some of us he would not be returning back to Northwest U. It saddened us all because we truly enjoyed the input he gave and added substance he brought in our classes of his perspective.

Two years later, Hal and I would re-connect through a mutual friend and now I am in the process of getting ready for the Mrs. Washington America Pageant. I was thinking of ways to really advertise and my friend suggested I ask Hal to work with me to create a promotional interview video. This was such an amazing idea and when Hal and I got together I was able to see yet another talent this young man had. Not only did he help me with my promotional video, he was the DJ for a fundraiser event I held to raise money for the pageant. Throughout the event, I kept checking in with Hal to see how he thought it was going. After the event, he said, "Jamicka you HAVE TO meet my sister." He had such a big smile on his face. I thought "sure I'll meet your sister." I didn't even know he had a sister because again, Hal is not a man of many words. He said I'm going to give you her information.

Stephanie and I met a few weeks later for coffee and after that, I pretty much ditched Hal and Stephanie became my new friend. Hal said I'd love her and we'd connect well and he was telling the truth. Stephanie took over from where Hal left off. She helped me come up with the letter concept of a 30 day Countdown to the Crown, which she constructed so beautifully for me. I mailed and hand delivered a copy of the letter to everyone I knew at the time. Many local businesses in the City of Fife, Milton, Puyallup, and Tacoma were very happy to support my endeavors. I exceeded my goal of raising $3000 in 30 days!

We talked for hours on the phone or communicated in other ways. She truly became my campaign manager and was there with me through to the end. She stopped what she was doing to help meet me find shoes to match a suit I was blessed with. The day we met up half way between Seattle and Fife we had a bite to eat with my two sons at Rain Forest Café. We probably spent too much time enjoying the roaring sounds of the animals in the Rain Forest before we proceeded on the mission to find shoes. The very first store we went into had the shoes. The shoes were a perfect match to the suit and we knew that was nothing but God -mission accomplished. We went our separate ways after the pageant, but still continued to stay in touch and find time in our lives to meet for lunch, dinner or coffee. Sometimes we'd go months without seeing each other, but we never have to explain why we haven't, we just pick up where we left off. She has been such an amazing friend in my life. Some years later she sent me the email you will read below. I've read it from time to time over the years and it continues to inspire and encourage me. I sent it to her just while in the process of completing this book and requested her permission to use it. She gladly replied, " OMG Yes! I couldn't have written it better today… it is the truth."

From: marie2323@aol.com [mailto:marie2323@aol.com]
Sent: Monday, August 31, 2009 2:18 AM
To: jamicka.jones07@northwestu.edu
Subject: Hey!

I don't know what God is up to or what you're up to...but I was washing my hair in my prayer closet/idea station (shower) and you kept popping in my head and these thoughts of you (below) keep popping up. I really felt the Holy Spirit compelling me to write this and give it to you now! It was one of those; you are not going to sleep until you do this task kind of things. You are really special to God; he loves you so much he had to track me down in the shower! I wrote the thoughts and felt like you know what this is about more than I do so this is what He laid on my heart! FYI this doesn't happen much but when it does it he always reveals to me I did the right thing. XOXO Steph

### (Words spoken through the Holy Spirit to Stephanie for delivery)

Jamicka is the epitome of greatness-a servant leader. Even though she has a pageant crown, she's always had one. We don't come by greatness and royalty often, but if you come to know this true woman of God you'll experience it.

*Jamicka is the kind of woman who will serve you greatly and in the next breath lead bravely. Just when you thought you have assisted her, you realize she helped you far above your expectations. She is bold enough to dream, brave enough to try, and worthy enough to succeed. Her beauty is captivating but like Jesus she'll wash your feet-literally and figuratively-because humility becomes her. Love is her essence, if you're not certain what love is or what it looks like or feels like, receive a hug from her and you'll clearly understand.*

*Joy resides in her eyes, her heart and her smile-if you've ever had a gloomy moment she'll wash it away and instill joy in your heart. The word of God says that if you want to be great in the Kingdom of God then you must serve. While so many of us struggle to be selfless, Jamicka is serving, giving, loving, caring & instilling joy-because of this she is leading!*

*Jamicka continue to dream and continue to press, what is yours!*

Ms. Stephanie Raines- Seattle, WA

## About the Book Cover Designer and Concept

One day in December 2013 working at Steilacoom High School, I found my way to Mr. Peter Johnson's Graphic Design class. I love to see what new artwork is displayed in the hall outside his room. The students at Steilacoom High School are so amazingly smart and very talented in so many different ways and I'm always in awe at what I see them do. I have strived to encourage each student I've had interaction with while working there.

Mr. Johnson caught me outside his room looking at the book covers the students re-designed from existing authors. I jokingly said, "Hey, I'm writing a book, they should design my book cover!" he smiled and said in his nice causal voice, "Sure". I thought to myself, "was he for real? Or was he joking right back with me?" He inquired more about me writing a book and I told him I had been thinking about it, but I planned to get working on it soon. He offered for his 2nd semester Graphics Design class to work on it as a project in the spring. I couldn't believe the opportunity that was taking place and the blessing God was giving me.

After that conversation, I thought about it and prayed about it and during Christmas break I began to strategize how to make it happen and what I wanted to talk about. I spoke to a few people and received some tips as well.

May 2014 one of Mr. Johnson's Graphic Design classes dedicated a few weeks on an assignment to create my book cover design. I wanted to give the students the freedom to be creative so I read an excerpt from my book, and the book synopsis and I told the students a little bit about myself. From that, there were some amazing book cover designs.

As Peter and I looked at the completed book cover designs, I was unaware of what student did what design. They were all so good that the decision was not an easy one. There was something extra special about Jamie Moul's.

Hers stood out to me and spoke to me and I believed represented not just the book, but who I am and all I strive to be.

Jamie Moul is from Fayetteville, North Carolina and is the oldest of six children. She has lived oversees for thirteen years attending various international schools. Jamie enjoys graphic design, drawing, star gazing, and playing sports. For the last seven years she has been active in swimming, soccer, basketball, and track. She also designed the cover for "The Dream Prison".

Mr. Peter Johnson's 3rd Period Graphic Design Class who all participated in the Book Cover Design Project in the Quest of my First Published Book — Taken June 2014

Selected Book Cover Designer - Jamie Moul & myself June 2014

## About the Author

Jamicka Jones was born in a south suburb of Chicago, IL. Her mother was able to walk away from her abusive drug addict and alcoholic father and at the age of 10, they packed up and moved to the small town of Savanna, IL. Her mother singlehandedly raised Jamicka and her two sisters working sometimes two jobs to make ends meet. Jamicka never allowed her circumstances to deter her from achieving any goal she has set. As a high school student maintaining a GPA of 2.0 she was persuaded to believe she would not make it into college. Thirteen years later, she proudly graduated with a Bachelor's Degree in Business Management from Northwest University. Throughout those thirteen years she fulfilled some major milestones and accomplishments.

In 1998 she joined the United States Army and was awarded two Army Accommodation Medals and an Army Achievement Medal. During her tour of duty she met her husband, Adon. The couple now have three sons; J'Don, Jamal, and Absalom. They reside in Lakewood, WA near Seattle.

While homeschooling J'Don and Jamal she participated in the Mrs. Washington America Pageant and was won Mrs. Congeniality 2009. Her most recent community activities include: member of the Diversity Committee for SHSD, Kiwanis of Steilacoom, Toastmasters International- City of Lakewood, WA, Washington Association of Educational Office Professionals (WAEOP), and National Association of Educational Office Professionals (NAEOP).

Although just starting her career as a motivational speaker, Jamicka has already begun to develop a good reputation for herself as one who will inspire, encourage, and engage an audience from high school students to educational and professional organizations to include Toastmasters International.

She is an energetic ball of fire that won't stop reaching for goals and achieving them. If you're looking for someone authentic, genuine, real, and that will leave you believing you can achieve anything; you've found her "I can do all things through Christ that strengthens me." Philippians 4:13

Myself with my 3^rd Grade Teacher- Mrs. Payne who is now the Principal at Coolidge Middle School in Phoenix, IL. Taken January 2014

At the Mrs. Washington America Pageant in Moses Lake, WA May 2009 with my family.

Visiting long time friend in VA, and my sister , nephew, and nephew drove from NC to visit. July 2013

Brienne and myself having fun at our Senior Prom together – April 1997

Made in the USA
Charleston, SC
13 November 2014